IN ALL MY SALT

ALSO BY ANNIE SOPHIE LE

The Absence of You

Bloom Under Moonlight

IN ALL MY SALT

ANNIE SOPHIE LE

Copyright © 2022 by Annie Sophie Le

All rights reserved.

No part of this book may be reproduced in any form or by any electronic or mechanical means, including information storage and retrieval systems, without written permission from the author, except for the use of brief quotations in a book review.

ISBN: 978-1-7775696-4-8

CONTENTS

More Salt Than Milk	1
Anger Is the God I Pray To	2
I Should Go to Therapy but I'm Broke	3
The Saltiness of Anger	4
Concrete Daisies	5
March	6
The Nature of Being Lost	7
Phantasm	9
Wife of Job	10
Petals	11
I Am Your Dinner	12
Too Sullied to Be Holy	13
More	14
Graveyard Life	15
For R	16
Yet Another Poem About Wormwood	17
In Which I Am Lady Macbeth	18
Forgiveness Is a Knife Without a Hilt	20
The Green House in Suburbia Where I Grew Up	21
Childhood Lessons	23
Mouthing Your Name	24
Milk From the Womb	25
I Am My Mother's Disappointment	26
A Neighbour Named Ester	27
A Quarter for a Mother's Lie	28
Tender Violence	30
My Triumph Is Not Hers	31
You Are Not My Mother Just Because You Birthed Me	32
A Mother's Love	33
Mother Dearest	34
Saying "The Parents Did Their Best" Is Just Another Excuse	36
Apparition	37
Curdled Milk from My Mother's Tit	38

I Mistake Violence for Love and Cruelty for Kindness	40
Forgiveness	41
This Is Where I Let You Go	42
Shared Blood Is Just Another Excuse	43
A	44
Forgiveness Does Not Mean Reconnection	45
What Are You?	46
My Ride-Sharing Driver Is an Asshole	47
Who I Am	49
Stuck	51
Bà	52
Bà II	53
Tender Cruelty	54
Ông	56
Family Portrait	57
A Good Man	59
A Good Man II	60
I Don't Want Anything From Him	62
Unwilling	63
"Were You Asking for It?"	65
High School	66
What Is Left Unsaid	68
Yet Another "Fuck You" Poem	69
So That's How It Starts, Right?	70
Ignition	72
I Am Not Responsible for His Loneliness	74
Friends Turned Strangers	76
Keeping a Wild Thing	77
Coffee Thoughts	78
Your Reflection	79
Pirate Ship	80
Together	81
Origami Hearts	82
Falling	83
Love Is an Apparition	84
Reverence	85
You're Too Much and I'm Not Enough	86
Breaking Up	87
Fevered	90
Love Can't Save Me	91

The Ending	92
Synthetic Words of Love	93
Empty Girl	94
Lemon and Apple	95
Hollowed Out	98
Hardness	99
The Girl Is an Object	100
I'm a Consolation Prize	101
Devoured	102
Embittered	103
Bones and Straw	104
Objectification by Wolves Is Just Another Way to Hate Myself	105
A Bed of Nails	106
The Only Way I Know How to Feel	107
Twigs and Bones	108
Cigarettes and Leftovers	109
Good Intentions	110
Sullied	112
I Leave Those Who Try to Love Me	113
Medusa	114
This Is the Last Poem About You	115
Wolverine Smile	117
It Takes Too Much Out of Me	118
More Than	119
My Worth Is Not Defined by My Productivity	120
Living Too Loudly for Such a Quiet Girl	122
Lazarus	123
I Won	125
Immeasurable	126
Self-Love Is Warfare	127
I'm Spiteful Enough to Still Be Alive	128
Spilling	129
Acknowledgments	131

MORE SALT THAN MILK

The innocence of milk,
the anger of salt—
it is here in these words
where the curdling begins.

ANGER IS THE GOD I PRAY TO

I found myself
in the spilling of my salt.

I SHOULD GO TO THERAPY BUT I'M BROKE

I need to release the anger
that salts my tongue—
anger is the only way I know how to heal—
but I'm not sure I want to hear
what my therapist will say,
though I already know the words:
*Annie, you can't sleep on a bed of nails
and call yourself healed.*

THE SALTINESS OF ANGER

I am bitterness,
I am anger.
I want to fight the world,
I want to fight my past.
Say *fuck you* to everyone who hurt me—
tell it to myself, too, for all the years
I tried to destroy myself,
leaving my life in tatters.
What do I do with this anger?
The need to dig and hurt and bleed.
Therapy is too expensive,
free group therapy,
too crowded and awkward.
This anger of mine, a burden,
a medal of honour that I survived,
is mine and mine and mine.
And yet, I want to hand it to others,
let them touch the jagged edges
and know this is who I am.
I bury it in my gut
and wrap myself in fine silks,
pretending I am healed.

CONCRETE DAISIES

I wonder why I'm so hard—
as if enduring were easy,
as if surviving made me softer
than petals.

MARCH

My condo building burned down this year,
and I lost thirteen years of my life
to a fire.
Displaced with nothing
but my dog,
three cats,
my father,
my phone,
and the clothes on my body.
I reeked of smoke
and shook from the trauma
of almost drowning in a sea of black smoke
when the ceiling ignited above us.
I'm bitter,
I'm annoyed,
I'm scared at the sound of a siren.
Now I live in an apartment
with loud screaming neighbours,
trying to rebuild thirteen years.
Going through the motions of trying to move on,
when all I want to do is go backwards.

THE NATURE OF BEING LOST

I am stuck in the middle,
between a roaring bear
and a raging river—
who I was and who I want to become.

I ask the bear
if I can stay on the shore with him,
and he tells me:
You do not belong with me.
I eat twisted little things like you
and pluck their bones from my teeth.

I ask the river
if I can swim in her arms,
and she tells me:
You will not make a home in me.
I drown hopeful little things like you
and fill their guts with jagged rocks.

I am stranded in the in-between,
holding onto the bear's fur coat
and letting my feet sink

into the rushing water—
of being here and being gone.

PHANTASM

The words don't come—
they are not here.
My tongue is missing—
where did I lose it?
In the spilling of my salt—
I guess I'm still angry.
And in the cupping of curdled milk—
forgiveness doesn't exist.
I fade from view,
a gruesome illusion
turned permanent.

WIFE OF JOB

When I look
behind me
at my past,
I turn into
a pillar of salt.

PETALS

My friends wonder
why I'm reserved.
As if trauma hasn't
taken my tongue.

My lovers wonder why
I flicker between hot and cold.
As if my brain could distinguish
between love and violence.

I wonder if there will
come a day when I'm not so hard.
As if I could pluck petals
from sunflowers,
glue them to my skin
and call myself healed.

I AM YOUR DINNER

My trauma is your dining room table.
Let's feast, you say.
Feast on this delightful feral girl
with chipped teeth
and enough anger
to feed a roomful of wolves.

TOO SULLIED TO BE HOLY

I wish I could be a fluttering butterfly
that catches people's eyes.
Delicate and beautiful
with tender glassine wings—
the sun glinting around me
as I dance in the air. Vulnerable
yet birthed from the bloody catastrophe
of ripping myself from a cocoon.
I wish I could be anything
but a burning tower,
crumbling and falling apart.
A moth obsessed with fluttering
to the flame of self-destruction.
I wish I could taste perfection,
instead of the wormwood of my anger.

MORE

With my roughened edges
and trauma perched on my shoulders,
with a crooked smile
and greasy hair,
I lose myself in daydreams
where I am more than myself.
More than my past,
more than my hurt—
more
more
more
—because I am still not enough,
but sometimes,
too much.

GRAVEYARD LIFE

My life is a cemetery,
filled with the ghosts of regrets
and the rotting flesh of lovers long gone.
And my friend tells me:
Annie, you can't make a home amongst dead things
and say you're living.

FOR R

I talk to this girl with glasses
and laughter too big for her body.
She is shy and hesitant to tell me
that she belongs to this club—
this unwanted shitty club
of survivors of abuse.
We used to spend hours
discussing her art and my poems,
but now we speak
in hushed voices about violence.
It is something we don't want to share,
but we do.
Something so many of us experience,
but we shroud ourselves in shameful silence.
I want to tell her the shame she carries is not hers,
help her douse her abuser's house in gasoline,
let it burn until nothing remains but pillars of ash.
But I don't, because anger is my road to healing,
and hers is beginning and filled with hurt.
If only she could see the strength in herself,
and how far she's carried herself to be here.
Despite the hardness which tried to break her,
she's here.

YET ANOTHER POEM ABOUT WORMWOOD

I realized yesterday
that my abusers still have power over me.
I know what you're thinking—let me explain.
I'm still angry,
still spilling salt and calling it healing.
Thinking about them
as I swim through the black tar
of hate that sticks to my skin.
I let them take root in my gut,
give them space in my head
as I chew on wormwood, trying to let go.
I thought anger was the road to healing
but I realize they're thriving,
and I'm still a shrivelled rage-filled thing.
Does this give them yet another victory?
How do I move on and let go,
while still telling them to go fuck themselves?

IN WHICH I AM LADY MACBETH

I was so used to the weight of silence,
I forgot how to use my voice.
I forgot how to speak.
I forgot I was alive.
I forgot.
I forgot.
I forgot.

And when I'm with my friend,
I'm rocking back and forth,
self-soothing.
Silent and thinking
about being anywhere,
but with her.

My friend reaches over
and grasps my hands,
telling me to stop being weird.
I stop breathing.
I stop moving.
I stop.
I stop.
I stop.

And I try to remember
what she was talking about.
I forgot to sprinkle
a word here and there
in the space between
the silence and her voice.

I want to hand her my anger,
and leave with my black coffee,
leave her sitting at the table—
alone—
with her chai latte.

She sees me getting up
and says:
I love you,
but look at what you're doing.

And I look down at my hands—
filthy—
from holding onto my trauma.

FORGIVENESS IS A KNIFE WITHOUT A HILT

I am so tired of people telling me to forgive.
Forgive those who have hurt me.
Forgive the boy who touched me.
Forgive her who I have sprung from
because of our shared blood.
Because
The past is in the past
and I should
Be the bigger person.
As though forgiveness is a gift I give away,
absolving them from what they've done.
As if I would carry their shame with me
when I would rather drown in an ocean of salt.

THE GREEN HOUSE IN SUBURBIA WHERE I GREW UP

green and white laminate tiles
cheap and tacky
crookedly laid

wooden spoon
smooth with age
swinging in the air

fresh flesh
young and soft

tender
tender
tender

smacking and pounding
on crescent peach skin
red moons blooming

pleas of mercy

the begging child
homeless tears

ragged and oily

here
here
here

there will be no peace
for wicked little children
my mother says

CHILDHOOD LESSONS

I learned as a child
that love is violent.
Smile for the camera and see
the cruel eyes between my parents.
There is no sanctity in marriage,
only lovers turned warring.
My sister and I,
wooden pieces on a chess board,
sliding forward
until the queen swallowed us whole,
and we tumbled down
between two parents,
pawns without a home.

MOUTHING YOUR NAME

I still can't say your name.
The thought of you,
still too much to bear.
The words are paper cuts on my tongue
when I try to speak your name.

When I remember your face,
I'm back to origami paper boats
floating in the muddy water
pooling in the ditch nestled against
the sidewalk outside our house,
which would occupy me for hours after it rained.

I tried to bury you deep in my bones,
clutched tightly at all the things
I thought I'd forgotten, wished I'd outgrown.

I hoped to bury you in the hollow of me
until one day, I'd wear a diamond crown
welded from childhood hurt and tears.

MILK FROM THE WOMB

How much curdled milk
from my mother's breast
did I swallow to become this hollow?

I AM MY MOTHER'S DISAPPOINTMENT

There is this woman,
who plucks hair from my head—
one strand at a time—
and sews a doll in my likeness
and fills it with straw.
She rips out my fingernails—
my hands raw and gnarled—
and glues them to the doll.
This doll is her child,
a projection
of who I am supposed to be.
The woman birthed this doll
from a waterfall of anguish and blood,
and she carries it around with her,
telling herself she did her best,
but there is only so much she could do
for a doll made from straw.

A NEIGHBOUR NAMED ESTER

When I was a child,
we had a next-door neighbour
who grew pink and yellow tulips in the spring,
nestled against her white picket fence
around her lush green yard.
I used to follow her around,
watch in childhood awe
as she watered her plants with kind hands.
I wanted to dig my heels into the buds
that demanded so much attention
away from me.
This woman, strange and ethereal,
so different from my mother,
with unending patience,
let me follow her around
as I wished I could have slipped from her belly.
She moved away, abandoning me,
this pretend mother of mine.
And as a child,
I wondered:
was I too much for her
or not enough?

A QUARTER FOR A MOTHER'S LIE

I stood in the bathroom
in my childhood home,
the green and white laminate floor
cold under my tense, curling toes.
My mother wrapped floss
around my loosening tooth,
and tied it to the doorknob.
She held the door open,
watching me cry and beg for her
not to slam the door shut.
The floss tasted of mint,
the tears mingling with the slime
running from my nose.
She promised she would count to three.
This oath of hers gave me courage,
my child heart believing
my mother would never lie to me.
I counted with her, but on two,
she slammed the door shut.
My little chipped tooth
ripped from my mouth.
I stared at her, disbelieving

this mother of mine had lied to me.
She held the tooth in the palm of her hand,
a trophy of my innocence;
and that night,
I was given quarters for my mother's lie.

TENDER VIOLENCE

Violence tastes the same as love
when the ones you love
hurt you and call it tenderness.

MY TRIUMPH IS NOT HERS

Sixteen with my life in trash bags,
the blame was settled upon my shoulders.
I was told I forced my mother's hand
when she kicked me out of my childhood home.
She said I was a wicked child,
an undeserving teenager
so far gone and unsalvageable,
who needed to be taught a lesson.
After I built myself up
from the stones and twigs of my trauma,
she took my trophy of survival,
crowned herself my saviour,
and told herself she was a good mother.

YOU ARE NOT MY MOTHER JUST BECAUSE YOU BIRTHED ME

There is no love, only guilt,
and when you die, I'll mourn
everything we could've been
but never were.
I often wonder if I should accept
you into my open arms,
and caress you with my love.
But I am not forgiving,
and I am worth more
than your castaway love.
I am only torn
out of duty and obligation
which connect our blood,
but I can easily deny
our shared marrow,
telling myself motherhood is earned.

A MOTHER'S LOVE

I was shown how to swallow my tongue,
and how to mute my mouth.
Learned love tasted the same as violence.
And years later, I still think it's normal
for a mother to teach her daughter
how to hate herself.

MOTHER DEAREST

She still blames me for being obstinate,
for the way she used to hit me,
forgetting the glass bowl
she threw at my head.

She blames me for the mess of a life
she made for herself,
and tells me it's my fault
for how she ended up like this.

She blames me for destroying
her body when she used to be beautiful.
As if a straw woman could
ever be beautiful.

This mother of mine
was never mine;
telling me she wished
she had aborted me.

I am the afterbirth
of her regrets and her anger.

Tearing at her breast
in search of warmth,
but only finding curdled milk.

SAYING "THE PARENTS DID THEIR BEST" IS JUST ANOTHER EXCUSE

You said they did their best
in raising a hellion of a child,
but that little slip of a girl
needed more
than they were willing to give.
Instead of teaching her love,
they taught her how to destroy herself.
And instead of preparing her
for the world, and shielding her from its thorns,
they built their empire of anger and locked doors
into a bed of nails for her to sleep on.
In place of the softness of love,
she grew from the hardness of anger
and the heaviness of silence.
This little slip of a girl,
disappeared into the walls,
hiding from thrown hands and cruel eyes.
Now tell me,
how did they do their best
when they were too busy hating each other
to cradle the children as they slept
and feed them milk and marrow?

APPARITION

How could you force a child to swallow
her tongue and teach her to be a cutting board
for strangers' knives? So when she grew up
into a ghost of a woman, she let herself
be eaten by wolves, mistaking it for love.

CURDLED MILK FROM MY MOTHER'S TIT

Some days,
I wonder if I made it all up.

The bruised peach skin.
The salt that fell from my eyes.
The nights of hunger in a locked room.

I remember the days
when we went swimming
and floated in the pool,
stinking of chlorine and sunscreen.

But then I remember
the glass bowl hurtling
towards my head,
the upturned table,
and the digging words.

I remember
sitting in a car hotter than an oven
and crying to be released.

I remember being told:

*I'm going to swallow
this whole bottle and crash the car.
I'll kill us all.*

I remember the pinching of my baby fat
and the faults found in my body—
a cage, a prison,
no longer a home for my guts.

I remember.

So I flicker
between false nostalgia
and the wormwood rooted in my bones,

and wonder,
how do I exorcise
a haunted past?

I MISTAKE VIOLENCE FOR LOVE AND CRUELTY FOR KINDNESS

I was delivered by a straw woman,
an offspring of her anger.
She roughed up my unripe flesh,
fed me my tongue in place of milk,
and taught me how to lose my limbs
to strangers' hands.
Amidst the raised voices and shaking fists,
I grew from the violence,
knowing no other way to be loved.

FORGIVENESS

Forgiveness is a word I'll never touch.
It is a flower I buried with you,
suffocating under the weight of the soil.
A rock in my pocket I carry with me,
weighing me down in the quicksand ground.
And even if I drown in an ocean of salt,
it is a word I'll never give you.

THIS IS WHERE I LET YOU GO

I won't give forgiveness to you,
and I don't want to hear your excuses;
that you were hurt as a child
and it's a vicious cycle.
I fall between thinking you
tried your best
and didn't try hard enough.
And in the gap between us,
there is still the salt of anger,
but instead of losing myself
to its edges, I know
I don't care enough about you
to carry you with me any longer.

SHARED BLOOD IS JUST ANOTHER EXCUSE

I still can't believe this man—the father
of my abuser—
told me that love is hard and love is painful,
and everything that happened to me
was done because I am weak.
That I always grow a mountain out of a grain of salt.
I sat there and stared at this twisted man
and thought,
So this is gaslighting.
But I nodded and remained silent.
(I was always good at being silent.)
It's been five years now,
and the idol worship I felt
for this old man has curdled our shared blood,
and turned me into a bitter, twisted hag.

A

I hate my full name
because it is too French
for my family to pronounce
in their strong Vietnamese accents—
a quiet violence
in every letter—
a cultural trauma,
a reminder
of a colonial past
and a gruesome divorce
between my parents.
I hate my name
because my mother chose it,
and every time
people say it,
I am reminded of her.

FORGIVENESS DOES NOT MEAN RECONNECTION

He lectures me on forgiveness,
saying I should stop being childish
and get over it.
But trauma wears my clothing,
and the roughness of my skin
can't let go.

She tells me to move on,
saying blood is thick
and won't curdle the milk.
But memories linger,
just as ink stains the skin.

They wonder why I remain quiet,
swallow my tongue and hold steadfast,
saving my tumbleweed words
for open ears
that don't demand reconnecting
with a cruel mother
and abusive men.

WHAT ARE YOU?

People ask me this,
always prefacing the question with:
I don't mean to offend you.
As though I won't take offence
to them questioning my ethnicity,
the depth of my skin tone,
the roundness of my eyes,
the exotic but plain features of my face.
They ask as though
they could better understand
how to categorize me,
questioning my authenticity
when I tell them I'm Vietnamese,
because
You don't look Asian
and
All Asians act differently than you.
As though I'm too much for them,
and yet,
not enough.

MY RIDE-SHARING DRIVER IS AN ASSHOLE

My brownness, my milkiness,
discomforts my ride-sharing driver.
He asks:
What are you?
as though I am an equation that needs solving,
my race an answer, a salve to his discomfort.
I'm petty, so I ask:
What do you mean?
Hoping to worsen his awkwardness,
and he shifts, his eyes back on the road,
but still, he repeats the question:
Are you Native?
As though Indigeneity was a slur,
an insult still used to colonize.
I am Vietnamese.
And he scoffs:
You don't look it.
And there it is.
The denial of my race,
my identity, and my ancestry.
I am often denied because of my appearance,
asked:
What are you?

As though my race matters more
than my bones and guts.
Somehow, I must look Vietnamese
to be Vietnamese,
and this logic has denied me
access to my heritage.
I am too white to fit in with my family
and culture. Too brown for society and racists.
I exist on the peripherals of each culture,
not fitting in wherever I go.
But I have learned to make space
for myself and come alive in that space,
exist however I want
and tell anyone who says otherwise
to fuck off.

WHO I AM

In my blood,
there is a land of rice paddies,
and sunshine-skinned herbs.

In my blood,
there is a land of white ash,
and mountain summits.

In my blood,
there are tales of wars survived,
and days fought.

My bones are etched
from ancestors who weaved
steel through the skins
of their families,
feeding open mouths
with a single grain of rice.

I am a daughter
from the lands of rice and snow.

I am a daughter
birthed from strength.

STUCK

My milk-stained brownness is
too light for half of my family,
too dark for the other half.
I am stuck,
here,
in the in-between,
a reluctant outsider,
a reminder of my parent's
bloody divorce,
in a family of commitments
and until death do they part.
This tribe of blood
that sees me
as grotesque and misshapen,
is not mine. I will not
find a home in their closed arms.
I will not find safety
in their barbed words
and rough hands.

BÀ

My grandma and I speak
in twisted hands and monosyllables.
Her Vietnamese tongue unable to form
English words native to mine.
And it's like this,
we spend a lifetime communicating
in half-words and a language of hands.

BÀ II

My grandma would babysit me,
her sprawled on the bed,
napping and exhausted
after spending her life
raising her children and grandchildren,
listening to Buddhist chants
from a rattling radio by her pillow.
I sat on the floor, the carpet a luscious cream,
looking at the pictures in a cookbook,
teaching myself how to bake bread,
as I mime the movements and eat the air.
Even now, twenty years later,
she asks me if I've eaten in broken English,
and I say yes, still chewing the air.
This is how we communicate,
my grandma and I.

TENDER CRUELTY

My family is sore
from rebuilding their bones
after leaving their home,
after the war,
after the dust settled,
after, after, after.

They carry trauma
in their blood,
just as they carry
their ancestors
in their veins.

My family is resentful
of each other,
of this world,
of this country
they now call home.

But this tribe of blood
still shares food
over a wooden table,
and reminisces

about the good
old days,
embalmed in fool's gold.

Generations of children
abide their elders,
not out of love
but out of duty,
and respect
that is expected
and not earned.

This is my family,
which despite the distance
between our houses,
still shares the same
skin and drinks
from the same cup.

A family in which
barbed words are hurled
between bites of food
drenched in fish sauce
hurting each other
and calling it love.

ÔNG

Today, I am dressed in my grandfather's shirt,
ill-fitting and slate blue.
And suddenly,
I am no longer missing him, I am him.
I am a workman, leaving Vietnam for Canada,
the patriarch of a too-big family
with a genial laughing smile.
This is how I try to hold onto the memories
of him. He's long passed and reborn into a crow
while I still look for his smile in strangers' faces.

FAMILY PORTRAIT

I was birthed from a man
with brown skin,
ravaged by war,
and a woman
made of porcelain
and madness.

My father left
the land of rice paddies
and sunshine-covered herbs,
for a concrete jungle
made of ice and cold.
My mother left
a home eaten
by hungry men
and a thankless family.

I am their daughter.
I am strength and madness.
I am brown and white.
I am tradition and modernity.
I used to try and exorcise
their blood from my veins,

hating myself because of them.

I used to rage against my marrow,
and the breast milk in my gut.
But though we share blood,
I am who I choose to be,
and I choose to be me.

A GOOD MAN

They call him a good man.
It's simpler still
to say he's the best of us.
But to a survivor who left
from under his thumb,
it's a mirage.
Others see the mirage during a drought,
cupping the sand in their hands
and thinking it is water.
Thirsty, they drink,
not realizing this water
will kill them.
But they are sinking into
the quicksand of loving him,
and they don't see
the violent quietness of him.
But they say he's a good man,
he's the best of us.

A GOOD MAN II

I remember the day after it happened—
when I learned the true nature of pain—
he never apologized to me.
He pulled me aside, and we sat down
on chairs made of nails,
and he recited a list of all the wrong things
I did and why I had forced
him to act that way.
Abusers will always blame the abused.

I don't remember too much of what he said—
why would I remember the taste of shit?
But the sinner never repented.
I sat there, muted and in awe
of this bully of a man with a silver tongue
and hateful eyes that lure so many
into believing he is a good man.

It's been six years now—
the road to healing is paved with anger—
and I wonder if there will come a day
when I won't chew on wormwood
and burn. But my anger is just—

just in that I did nothing wrong
and he hurt me because he could.

It was not my fault, and I am not to blame—
it took me too long to realize that—
and the shame I once carried
from his violence is not mine to carry.
I replaced the ocean of shame
with salt, and it keeps me afloat.

I DON'T WANT ANYTHING FROM HIM

Because of the gaslighting, sometimes I
doubt it was all that bad. I only
want him to acknowledge the scars
he left behind, the flinching of my shoulders
when I am scared, the unresolved anger
when others tell me it wasn't that bad,
the smallness of my voice when I am hurt.
But then I think, I want nothing from him.
I do not want his name in my mouth.
I do not want his name in my ears.
An apology was all I wanted,
but I would rather have him
fall down a flight of stairs
because I am spiteful and anger
is the only way I heal.

UNWILLING

Look at a skirt—
drown in a sea of shame.
It'll take years
to wear a skirt again,
without irony,
without wanting to be used,
without hating every moment of it.

You'll go through therapists
and friends who place
the blame at your feet,
and tell you that
you earned the assault,
because you were friends,
and friends always consent,
and being silent is just
another way of consenting,
and you didn't protest
loud enough, and shoving
his hands away wasn't good
enough.

And even now,

you don't speak of it.
Instead, you shrug it off
and minimize it, call
yourself healed and over it.
So when you finally
put words to the acts,
and stop hiding behind
monosyllables and half-truths,
naming it for what it is,
owning your truth,
you aren't ashamed anymore.

You're angry, you're pissed,
and you wonder,
how dare he treat your body
as a commodity
he felt entitled to.

You want to burn his house down
and tell yourself it's enough
for a lifetime of shame.
You want to be a whale
and swallow the salted world whole
and spit out his bones.

Violence is the only way to let go,
and you'd burn the world to ash
for a chance to heal.

"WERE YOU ASKING FOR IT?"

My old friends protested my confession—
my spoken truth—
telling me
it was my fault.
I was asking for it.
How could anyone believe me,
this lost girl with dirty hair.
His parents rich, mine poor.
They saw our friendship
as an excuse for him buying me—
colonizing my skin and calling it his.
They said he had every right
to leave oil-stained fingerprints
on my teenage skin.
When my *No* wasn't loud enough,
because *No* means *Yes*,
and *Boys will be boys*.

HIGH SCHOOL

That year,
we munched on razor blades and secrets
whispered between cupped palms and rosy cheeks.

We wore clothing too big
in stark black and monochrome greys,
the shirts swallowing our budding teenage bodies.

We were ghosts haunting the hallways,
swapping stories of how we were tired
from staying up too late, chatting online with strangers
past midnight.

We barely ate, surviving on gossip and angst,
pretending to hate boys, pretending to hate ourselves.
There were promises sworn over twisted fingers,
promises we forgot the next day.

We were best friends,
this girl with curly brown hair.
She tried so hard to be as mad as me,
but she was too sweet to turn herself
into a twisted little thing.

We fell out of each other's arms the next year,
when she blamed me for my assault,
angry that I would lie about a boy she liked.

But I'll never forget that year,
the year we spoke in daydreamed whispers,
promising forever and a day.

WHAT IS LEFT UNSAID

Maybe if I don't speak the words,
the sexual assault wasn't real.
The only way I can move forward
is through self-destruction and poems
where I tell myself I'm healed.
But healing is just another magic trick—
that is to say,
magic doesn't exist,
and miracles are delusions
for the hopeless romantics.
I don't believe in either,
so maybe I'm not healed—
just moved on in a twisted way.
A wreckage turned monument.
Once a pretty little girl
now venomous and feral.

YET ANOTHER "FUCK YOU" POEM

My silence was not my consent.
My smile was not my permission.
My skirt was not an invitation.
My friendship was not a green light.
I am not an object for you to buy.
My body is not yours to colonize.
I don't owe you affection,
and though you did your best
to eat me whole,
I survived.

SO THAT'S HOW IT STARTS, RIGHT?

His grin, wide and smug.
His outstretched hands touching
and reaching, meant to disarm
the protests. This man feels
entitled to women's bodies,
to colonize them and call it
consensual. And when even slapping
his hands away and telling him *No*
excites this shit of a man—this man
so used to hearing silence as a *Yes*—
he takes what he wants and leaves
only twigs and shame behind.
He tells himself he did nothing wrong.
The women were asking for it, wanting
a piece of him and they never
fought hard enough, so why does it matter?
The women's bodies are a battlefield,
and society will blame them,
telling them that *Boys will be boys*
and to shut up about the assault—
it's not polite conversation.
Don't chisel the assault

into a coffee table for all to see
and call it healing.

IGNITION

It took me years
to be able to speak of you,
fearing I again would hear:
What were you wearing?
Were you asking for it?
You're making a big deal out of nothing.
It never happened.
Stop lying.

And in therapy
when I told a roomful
of strangers about you
and your rich family,
they believed me.
Only one person
asked why
I never told anyone
before.

I am tired of the memories
of your hands on me,
tired of remembering
the way your eyes lit up

when I struggled.

I used to cry at the sight
of skirts.
And the next year,
after the assault,
I wore blankets for clothing,
and you transferred
to a different school,
leaving only your fingerprints behind.

Out of spite,
I met men who used me
and forgot about me
after the lust cooled.

And out of spite,
I write this poem,
telling my truth
and hoping your house
burns to the ground.

Anger is just another word
for healing,
and in these words,
I ignite, burning those
who take too much.

I AM NOT RESPONSIBLE FOR HIS LONELINESS

He sends me dick pics
and emojis of winking yellow faces—
obscene and unsolicited—
asking what I would do
if I were there with him.
As if I only exist to worship his body,
only there for his pleasure.

He hints—in not-so-subtle ways—
of how I owe him
for changing my mind years ago,
when we first met.
I had promised to fuck him
but changed my mind.
I'm not allowed, he says. *I owe him.*

And he invites me over to his apartment,
over and over and over,
not accepting my declines,
ignoring my silence.

I stopped talking to this man,
who demanded ownership

of my body and wanted to eat me—
bones and all—
and I can feel his anger
at my disappearing act,
a magic trick, the last *fuck you*
I wanted to say.

I do not owe him anything,
but I am afraid for the women
he will meet and cleave apart.
Colonizing women's bodies—
the only way he knows how to love.

FRIENDS TURNED STRANGERS

I don't talk about my relationships with my friends,
holding pieces of myself back from them.
Letting them think I am eternally single,
a hopeless cause, a boring girl with no use for romance.
I barely know how to hold a conversation with them;
letting them chat over me, filling the air
between our mouths with their words,
their lives too full and vibrant,
mine too empty and dull.
Why are they friends with me?
Why do they like me
when I don't even like myself?

KEEPING A WILD THING

I trace constellations
in the hollows above your collarbone,
drawing forget-me-nots
between the river of freckles
on the plane of your skin.
You slide from between my arms,
slip into the ink-stained night,
leaving no trace of you behind.
This is my penance—
it was my mistake
for trying to keep you.

COFFEE THOUGHTS

I found a home in you,
but what the hell was I thinking,
finding a home
in such an
empty place?

YOUR REFLECTION

I fell in love with the idea of you.
My heart a waterfall,
crashing and loud in its earnestness.
When I left you,
I broke my own heart,
realizing I loved the idea of you,
more than I did you.

PIRATE SHIP

He smells of apples
left too long in the sun
like shrunken and shrivelled
laughing heads, sweet and rotting.
His beard is too long,
his hair uncombed and dishevelled.
I want to lose myself
in his body and smiling eyes,
but I twist my fingers
in muted yearning under my thighs
to keep from sandpapering
him with my edges.
I betrayed myself,
falling for this strange man.
And suddenly—
watching him and wanting him—
I'm on a plank on a pirate ship
with my mutineer's heart.

TOGETHER

Even together,
there is still loneliness.

ORIGAMI HEARTS

We make shadow puppets with our intertwined hands
beneath the bladed half-moon, weaving our love story
around the sharp stars. Let the night deliver us.
Let our hearts shelter us when the rain weeps
from the clouds, splattering against our bedroom window.
We were once lost by ourselves, but let us be lost
together. Let the origami shadows dance around us,
from promises made by our tangled fingers.

FALLING

With your crooked smile
and sparkling eyes,
you were worth the heartbreak.

LOVE IS AN APPARITION

It is empty notebooks on a writer's shelf
that will never be filled, just hoarded.
It is a poem I write to you,
sitting on my bed with my sleeping dog beside me
staring at the screen and wondering
why some days the words come easily,
and other days I strain
but can't force them from my fingertips.
It is a spark that burns like light
but dims into a steady pulse.
Love is an apparition in a haunted house,
and I often get lost in thoughts of you,
in the curves and waves of your every smile.
It is the belief that your love will catch me
as I free-fall from the clouds
but then there is disappointment
that not even your love
can save me from falling from the air.
Oh, how I wish your love could save me.
How I wish love could save us all.

REVERENCE

The sanctity of the closeness of our bodies,
so beautifully undone, so wholly full.
We move together, a communion of the wildness
of our flesh.

Fingers weave above our heads,
a crowning of togetherness, our skins swimming
in an ocean of sweat.

We speak in a language of dancing bodies,
drinking holy water from each other's mouths.

Sacrosanct pleasure hums in our singing blood,
and we lose ourselves in the worshipping
of our shared holiness.

YOU'RE TOO MUCH AND I'M NOT ENOUGH

Your silence—so loud it burns my ears.
I slide my hands under my thighs,
wanting to reach over and trail
my fingers over the crinkles
at the corners of your eyes,
weathered braille I'll miss.
This is over—the words bitten
between the white tombstones in your mouth.
You wanted more than I could give you,
I wanted less than you gave.
It's for the best, I say, relieved I can go back
to my self-imposed exile,
away from your demanding hands.
We part on good terms, quietly fading
from each other's lives.
My friends don't ask about you—
they didn't know there was an 'us'.
I never spoke of you,
ashamed of myself for falling
for a tree of a person,
your roots too stable
beneath my earthquake feet
and manic brain.

BREAKING UP

When I am weak and want to beat myself up
over losing the good times,
I go through pictures on my phone,
digging and sifting,
finding lost relics of us.
When I was enough for you.
When I loved you.
When we were happy.

I study them, an anthropologist cataloguing
every wide smile and posed hug.
I used to send them to you with emojis
because words are too hard sometimes,
especially when words aren't enough.
When words could break
the fragile acceptance
of mutual love and mutual loss.

You used to reply:
I miss you.
I miss us.
Those were good times.

Then you stopped replying
and I stopped texting.
Deciding enough was enough
and some memories should stay buried,
not paraded around to remind myself
of lost times, of how much we've changed—
how much we've lost, when we gave up on us—
and let the distance grow
in the canyon between our hearts.
When you replaced me in your life
and I filled the absence of you
with wildflowers and wild words.

Now, when we bump into each other,
we're just strangers,
navigating through tense and awkward words:
How are you?
I'm fine.
You used to say:
We'll go out sometimes.
We'll catch up.
And foolishly, I believed you,
waiting around all Sunday for your texts
and last-minute plans, but they never came,
and I stopped waiting.

I've stopped excavating my phone,
letting time eat the pictures.
And I don't miss us
or the times we would stay up all night,
staring into each other's eyes
and laughing into the early mornings.
Not even pictures can erase
how you wandered from my life
when I was ill,
when I was no longer fun to be around.

I don't miss us,
and I don't miss you.

FEVERED

Our love was bigger than our bodies,
but it was never meant to last.

LOVE CAN'T SAVE ME

Your bomb shelter heart
lured me into your arms,
and I wanted to find
safety in you,
but all I found was
my heart cleaved in half
when I foolishly thought
you could save me
from myself.

THE ENDING

With a flick of a finger, you leave me.
Once starstruck lovers turned bitter rivals.
You sand your teeth into sharp edges,
your cutting tongue in your mouth.
And when we hug our farewells
in outstretched rigid arms,
our hearts withdraw from our sleeves
and curdle from the bitterness
in the space between us.

SYNTHETIC WORDS OF LOVE

I missed you,
she says with her wide smile
and crinkled eyes,
but I've been so busy.
And the memories of our togetherness
vanish behind the lids of my eyes.
I don't see my reflection in her face,
don't feel lost in her mossy green eyes,
and as we sit across from each other,
bitter steaming americano
burning the tip of my tongue,
eating the lining of my stomach,
I don't feel anything for her anymore.
With her sweet words,
she had colonized my heart, forced
her way in, wrapping herself around me
until I had scraped the meat from my ribcage
to make room for her in my gut.
That was then, but faced
with the apparition of our love,
I accepted that she was
too busy for me,
too busy fucking him.

EMPTY GIRL

I've scraped myself clean for you
until not even my ribs remain.

LEMON AND APPLE

At our favourite diner we used to haunt,
we sit together but apart,
a scarred wooden table bolted
to the carpeted floor between us.

We try to decipher each other's faces,
reaching out to trace the braille and folds
on our palms.
Our sighs are the conversation
we can't seem to have.

The server comes and takes our orders,
lemon water for me, apple pie for you.
She asks if I'm on a diet,
this stranger—an intruder and a witness—
during our last meal together.

You look away as I smile at her,
No, I'm not hungry, I reply,
and she saunters off, leaving us to our funeral
where we stare at our relationship's end
and wonder where we went so wrong.

You turn back to me and the earth quakes,
cracks forming beneath our feet.
I let my smile slide
into the growing crevasse between us.

You eat silently,
I sip my iced lemon water warily.
The memories of hours spent talking
into each other's mouths
are sandpaper rubbing against my skin.

You slide money onto the table, paying for your pie,
a transaction for the last hour of 'us.'
And we bury our dead,
casualties of our war which lasted months.

So this is the end of our togetherness;
my empty gut full of sour, your endless hunger
satiated from sugar-laden apples.

I could never give you what you wanted.
I was never enough,
but some days, I was too much.

A manic muse, a depressed artist.
Too loud and too quiet.
Flighty and moody.
Needy but distant.
Too hard to love.
So easily bruised.

We stare at the tombstone
etched with the dates of our relationship,
a love turned burial ground,
separating ourselves from each other.

We leave the diner and walk down the sidewalk
in different directions.
And while you mourn over what we lost,
I mourn over wasted time.

HOLLOWED OUT

Writer's block,
writer's block,
Sahara desert mind.
I gave you all of my words
and left none for myself.

HARDNESS

Love is a quiet thing,
a sunflower blooming under the sun.
I was a rose, covered
in thorns, and this strange man
came around,
clipped the thorns from my skin.
And I found myself
sheltered in kind hands.
So foreign, this feeling of warmth.
So sudden, this rush of love.
I bristled against him, trying to destroy
everything he gave me.
How else could I survive
this man carved from kindness,
when I am harder than stone,
too rough to love?

THE GIRL IS AN OBJECT

I love the heartbreak
more than the love.
And I walk around
searching for those
who will hurt me,
pulling away
from those with kind smiles.
I want the pain
more than the tenderness.
And the thrill
of being wanted
is better than sex.

I'M A CONSOLATION PRIZE

An easy target for strangers
who are desperate,
but not as desperate as I am.
Strangers who are lonely,
just as lonely as I am.
And even together, there is still space
between our bodies, space
where self-loathing and regret
grow and bloom into a twisted garden.
Another dead flower
in my bouquet of self-destruction.

DEVOURED

The first time I had sex,
it was awkward and filled with his grunts.
It hurt to sit down for a week afterwards,
and my skin burned from his sandpaper hands
when I came home and showered his smell off me.
I didn't say no, does that still matter?
I should've walked away but let him take
too much of my guts and bones,
leaving only skin and teeth behind.
Obedient like a bitch in heat,
letting him slap and bite me
until my peach-skinned flesh tore.
Years later, I still think of him.
When it's too quiet, the night too still,
wondering why it felt so good to be torn apart,
why it felt so good to be used.
Is this self-destruction,
another way to hate myself?
Or is this the only way I know
how to feel something,
other than cutting myself to shreds?

EMBITTERED

Bitterness sits on my tongue,
and I tell myself what an orchestra
I am building
from a few twigs turned violins.
But instead of invalidating what I feel,
I embrace the roughened emotions,
and try not to tear myself to pieces
over someone who wants all of me,
leaving nothing left for myself.

BONES AND STRAW

A dime store girl ready to be bought
by men who bare their teeth
and cut with their roughened hands.
A straw girl turned prey,
empty
empty
empty
waiting to be filled,
pillaged until nothing remains but bones.

OBJECTIFICATION BY WOLVES IS JUST ANOTHER WAY TO HATE MYSELF

This is how I come home,
covered in fingerprints and tousled hair.
A sticky mess between thighs
and skin reddened from sloppy kisses.
I don't know what it feels like
to be wanted for myself,
instead of being objectified
for the flesh between my thighs.
So I cut myself to pieces—
digestible little nuggets—
easy to be feasted upon by predators
who tell me I'm pretty.
It's a game I play with myself,
letting strangers fill me—
and telling myself that trauma
didn't turn me into this empty girl
with paper-cut skin,
who only feels something
when being used—
so desperate to be reborn.

A BED OF NAILS

I read poems about love,
gentle and alluring, soft as petals,
and wonder why it tastes so bitter to me.
I only find wormwood affection and bitten words
that hold no truth.
I am a commodity, a silent rag doll of a girl
who lets her body be colonized
as she hates herself.
I write about the joy in my anger
and the hope in my sadness.
I can't write love poems without tragedy,
only having tasted melancholic kisses
and crowded loneliness.
Even here, even now,
I write and write and write,
but the only love I find
is hard and fast,
and sharp as nails.

THE ONLY WAY I KNOW HOW TO FEEL

I remember every stranger
and keep their ghost
in the cavern in my chest,
becoming a haunted house,
my skin covered in tombstones.
I use their names to write poems
about self-destruction.
A cartographer mapping
every mountain grown
upon a mound of trauma.
I let the strangers use me
because being used
is just another way
to make myself feel.

TWIGS AND BONES

Comparing every stranger
to the man who took too much
and left little behind.
Wondering just how much
these wolves will hurt me,
how much of myself
I have left to give,
when there is
so little of me to take.

CIGARETTES AND LEFTOVERS

I am bloated
from the leftovers of yesterdays,
and my mouth is bloody and raw
from eating the cigarette butts
from men who rut in me
and call it love.

GOOD INTENTIONS

When I was twenty-six,
I almost burned my kitchen to the ground,
forgetting the pan of oil heating
on the stove.
My apartment filled with a fog of smoke,
the air turning black and acrid,
staining the walls.

My cats and dog ran around—
wild—
as I corralled them
into a cage,
one of them hiding.
I never found him
until after the firefighters left,
cowering under my bed.

My floor was piled with dirty clothing,
bras
and
underwear,
and when the firefighters came
they stepped all over my underwear

and saw the make-up
smeared
all over my face.

It took me days to scrub
the smoke from the walls,
and I still find streaks
I missed,
seven years later.

My family asked me
how the hell could I forget
a pan of oil
on the stove
as I tried to cook them dinner.

And I told them:

My good intentions
always end in tears
and men walking all over
parts of me.

SULLIED

I don't believe in miracles,
only sleight of hand
and secrets between con artists.
And if I pray to God,
does Heaven exist?
Or is it something
I only want to believe in
when I'm hollowed out,
too covered in dirty fingerprints
to be a holy church?

I LEAVE THOSE WHO TRY TO LOVE ME

and fall in love
with strangers
and whisky men
who smell of stale cigarettes.
Men who step on me
and fuck me with rage,
leaving my cooling body
to my lonely regrets.
Is this the only way I feel,
fucking tin men
and calling it love?

MEDUSA

I seek out men
who move like wolves and taste of danger.
I don't look for softness or kind words,
only those who will use and forget me.
They see my sharp smile—more baring of teeth—
and mistake my feral silence for need.
I've swallowed my anger, carried it in my gut,
let them touch me, my fellow conspirator
in fucking myself apart.
Some days,
I call this moving past my trauma,
and other days,
I call this another way to destroy myself.
But today, I feed my hair made of snakes
with their greed
and call it
freedom.

THIS IS THE LAST POEM ABOUT YOU

I've decided to stop
thinking about you,
wasting ink on you,
giving you a home on too many pages,
letting your ghost haunt me.

I don't know what forgiveness is,
and even if I did,
I don't think I'd be able to give it to you.
But if I keep holding on to the past,
not letting dead things stay buried,
I'll lose myself.

I don't want to be angry anymore.
I don't want to remain rooted
in the hurt,
I want to move on from you.
So this is it—
this will be the last thing
I'll ever give you.

I'll let go and release you in the wind

and breathe in peace.
I will bloom,
and I will be happy.

WOLVERINE SMILE

I am ugly,
not because of my skin or face
but because of the trauma in my gut
and the baring of my teeth
when you tell me to smile.

I am ugly,
not because my fatness or flakiness
but because of the bitterness in my marrow,
and my hair ignites in flames
when you tell me to move on and get over it
so I can be pretty again.

I am ugly,
but in my ugliness,
I've never been more beautiful.

IT TAKES TOO MUCH OUT OF ME

Not being enough
and being too much.
Not being good enough
but good enough for me.
Happy I'm alive,
but unhappy I'm not living.
Stuck here in the space I take up
but not knowing where I belong.
And in the space between
fuck this and *fuck them*,
I build myself a straw hut
from twigs twisted from tornadoes of madness
and clay slick from hurricanes of trauma.
Something holy and for myself.
And even if it burns to the ground,
I'll build sandcastles from the ashes,
and call it home.

MORE THAN

Let them believe
I have nothing left to give.
Let them assume
I am nothing more than
the trauma I sprung from.
Let them deem me unworthy
because of the madness in my brain.
Let them shake their heads
at the anger that reddens my blood.
Let them.
Let them.
Let them.
But they will never
take away my voice.

MY WORTH IS NOT DEFINED BY MY PRODUCTIVITY

Do they care
who I am
when I have
nothing left to give?

Am I worthless
when my hands
are missing?

They can take
all that I am,
harvest my skin
into a leather jacket
for them to parade
around.

But my worth
is not defined
by society or
men in power.

My worth
is in the flowers

which bloom
between the cracks
in my hardness
and my willingness
to keep growing
through what
I go through.

LIVING TOO LOUDLY FOR SUCH A QUIET GIRL

I am too much for myself.
Too much
that not even my skin
can hold me together.

LAZARUS

I have
a voice made of thorns
and I will rise.

My body takes up
too much space
but I will use that space
and be heard.

My worth
is not defined
by my productivity.
I am more
than society's token.
I am more
than their trophy.
Synthetic caring from strangers
will not speak on my behalf.

I eat their words
and tell them:
You will not define me
so you will be comfortable

with my brownness.
You will not disenfranchise my colour
to keep your status quo.

In their peripherals,
I will rise
and I will speak.

I WON

my brownness—
milk-stained coffee

my tattoos—
a battlefield of times lost and won

my scars—
a walking masterpiece of fucking up

my trauma—
paper cuts on my bones

my life—
mine mine mine

IMMEASURABLE

Don't cry, just be strong, they tell me.
As though my strength is only measured
when holding back a tidal wave of tears.
They don't realize that my strength is immeasurable.
I have survived firestorms, and a tsunami of tears
threatening to drown me.
I have endured a tornado of self-destruction,
whipping me around.
I have come this far and still, I face the day
knowing I will fall again.
But I follow the trail of hope
and with grace,
I will dust away the sadness and get back up.
For I have survived and blossomed
through the cracks in the concrete.
I will survive,
I will overcome,
and in that,
they cannot measure me.

SELF-LOVE IS WARFARE

Weaponizing words of self-growth,
I rise with snaked hair,
chewing on wormwood,
tongue ignited.
My hardness cracks
from a wildflower garden,
bursting from defiance.

I'M SPITEFUL ENOUGH TO STILL BE ALIVE

I want to tell
everyone who hurt me
to fuck off.
I want to light
their houses on fire,
and call it healing.
I survived,
despite their best attempts
at destroying me.
I am here.

SPILLING

With a snaked tongue,
I will rise
and eat the world.
I will burn
and come alive
in the salt that I spill.

ACKNOWLEDGMENTS

Thank you to my editor, Misti Wolanski, for your care and compassion with this poetry collection. It has been a wild ride in the years we've worked together and I'm forever grateful to you. Thank you Kit Good, for your care and thoughtfulness with this collection.

Bô, thank you for being steady, and for your constant support and love. When I say I couldn't do any of this without you, I mean it. I don't know where I'd be without you. I love you.

Thank you to my friends for your presences in my life, and your love when I wasn't kind to myself. I love you.

Thank you, dear reader, for your support and for reading this collection. It was hard to face my trauma, even harder to put words to it, but the experience was freeing. *In All My Salt* is both the beginning of facing my past and the end of giving space to my abusers and the trauma. It is letting go and moving forward.

What I learned writing this collection is what I will share with you now: we are not our trauma, we are not defined by what we went through, and we are worthy in the space we take up.

In Salt,
Annie Sophie Le

www.anniesophiele.com
Instagram: @anniesophiele

www.ingramcontent.com/pod-product-compliance
Lightning Source LLC
Chambersburg PA
CBHW030304100526
44590CB00012B/508